Captain John Paul Jones
AMERICA'S FIGHTING SEAMAN

Also by Ronald Syme

ILLUSTRATED BY WILLIAM STOBBS

Alexander Mackenzie, Canadian Explorer
Balboa, Finder of the Pacific
Captain Cook, Pacific Explorer
Cartier, Finder of the St. Lawrence
Champlain of the St. Lawrence
Columbus, Finder of the New World
Cortes of Mexico
De Soto, Finder of the Mississippi
First Man to Cross America
Francis Drake, Sailor of the Unknown Seas
Francisco Coronado and the Seven Cities of Gold
Francisco Pizarro, Finder of Peru
Garibaldi, The Man Who Made a Nation
Henry Hudson
John Smith of Virginia
La Salle of the Mississippi
Magellan, First Around the World
The Man Who Discovered the Amazon
On Foot to the Arctic, The Story of Samuel Hearne
Quesada of Colombia
Sir Henry Morgan, Buccaneer
Vasco da Gama, Sailor Toward the Sunrise
Walter Raleigh
William Penn, Founder of Pennsylvania

ILLUSTRATED BY RALPH RAY

Bay of the North, The Story of Pierre Radisson

ILLUSTRATED BY JACQUELINE TOMES

African Traveler, The Story of Mary Kingsley
Nigerian Pioneer, The Story of Mary Slessor

Captain John Paul Jones
AMERICA'S FIGHTING SEAMAN
by Ronald Syme
illustrated by William Stobbs

William Morrow and Company   New York

The rich green fields, bordered with white-flowered hawthorn, sloped down to the golden yellow sands of Scotland's Solway Firth. The glow of the setting sun sparkled on that broad inlet of the sea and on the brown canvas sails of the fishing boats. Away to the south, the coastline of northwest England was visible across the water. 1442580

The high, slate-roofed house of Mr. John Craik stood on a low green headland overlooking the Solway. Mr. Craik was proud of the splendid view from his front windows. He was very nearly as proud of his magnificent garden, surrounded by a lofty stone wall, at the rear of the house. If Mr. Craik had any grievance at all, it was that his Scots gardener, John Paul, was a most obstinate man. Every time Mr. Craik wanted to plant apple trees, Paul suggested pear trees instead. The gardener also insisted that the summerhouse Mr. Craik was building have a round shape rather than a square one.

"Do you think you know more about gardening than I?" Mr. Craik angrily inquired of him one day.

"No," replied Paul in his serious manner. "But you engaged me as a *landscape* gardener, and landscaping doesn't mean planting everything in straight lines or squares, like a lot of marching soldiers."

John Paul nearly always had his own way in

the end. He was an extremely capable man, and Mr. Craik was well aware that a number of his wealthy neighbors would be very glad to secure Paul's services for the gardens on their own estates.

In his white-walled gardener's cottage, Paul did not have his own way so successfully. His wife, Jean MacDuff, who had been born in the neighboring village of Arbigland, was a busy, competent, and strong-willed little woman. Jean was an excellent cook and housekeeper, and she thriftily looked after her husband's wages. She also cared for their four children, William, Mary, Janet, and John, feeding them on porridge, fresh meat, milk, and vegetables from the garden.

The last child, John Paul, had been born July 6, 1747. Before he was old enough to walk, John was showing signs of becoming as obstinate as his father.

Ten years later, the sandy-haired boy, with

eyes of a strange hazel color, was even more independent in his ways. His favorite hobby was fishing offshore in a small dinghy. Often barefooted, and tanned a golden brown by sun and wind, John allowed only his special friends to accompany him on these trips. Before stepping into the boat, they had to promise not to complain of the cold, or get seasick, or clamor to return home before John's basket was filled with the freshly caught dabs and flounders that he was after.

Any companion who ever broke a rule was never allowed to fish with him again. "Go and play with the girls," John would say bluntly to any boy who displeased him. "You're of no use to me in a boat."

Even in those early days, John's direct manner of speech lost him some friends. Classmates at the little local school in the village of Kirkbean were either his firm supporters or his angry enemies. The Reverend James Hogg,

the schoolmaster, regarded sturdy John Paul as a clever and highly intelligent boy, but one who had to be kept constantly under strong discipline.

Soon after his fourteenth birthday, in 1761, John packed a couple of woolen jerseys, two pairs of stout homespun pants, some socks, and a spare pair of well-cobbled shoes into a sea chest. After saying good-bye to his parents, and receiving a parting present of a golden guinea from Mr. Craik, John Paul went off to sea.

His first vessel was the little two-masted brig *Friendship*, about to sail for the West Indies. As usual, England was at war with France, but he was not scared by the fact that the *Friendship* might be captured by the enemy. Nor was he upset by the thought that his apprenticeship would last seven years, during which time his wage would never be more than five shillings per week. John Paul merely wanted to go to

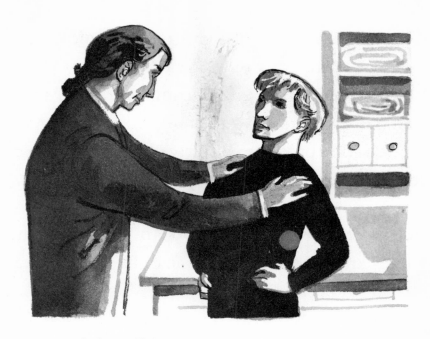

sea, and he did so in the simplest and most direct manner.

The *Friendship* went first to the West Indian island of Barbados, where she picked up a cargo of rum and sugar and took it to Hampton, Virginia. In the growing town of Fredericksburg John visited his older brother William, who was beginning to prosper as the town's leading tailor. Then his ship sailed back to England with another cargo of tobacco, pig iron, and sheaves of sawn boards, which were to be used for making barrels.

Paul learned his seamanship the hard way, and he learned it well. The Atlantic Ocean, he found, could be bitterly cold and mercilessly rough, and the American coast was often an invisible menace during rainstorms, fog, and blizzards. The Caribbean Sea, with its shoals and hurricanes, was as dangerous as any stretch of ocean in the world.

When, in 1764, the owner of the *Friendship* went bankrupt, seventeen-year-old Paul was released from his apprenticeship. For a number of reasons, however, he had no difficulty finding new employment at sea on another ship.

John Paul had taught himself a great deal by reading endlessly and practicing the art of writing letters. He had also lost his broad Scots accent and learned to speak English correctly. Arithmetic and higher mathematics apparently were no problem to him, after the good grounding he had received in those subjects from the Reverend James Hogg. During his three years aboard the *Friendship* he had shown he was honest and careful in the handling of money. And, most important of all, he was already a reasonably good navigator.

From the *Friendship* he went to the *King George,* a slaver running between the West African coast and the West Indies. Aboard this harshly run and detestable ship he proved himself a capable junior officer. Two years later, at nineteen years of age, Paul became chief officer on another slaver, the ill-named *Two Friends.*

John Paul hated this trade, the carrying of wretched human cargo. "It is an evil business," he wrote. "I left the abominable commerce as soon as I found alternative employment."

13

The little two-masted vessel *John,* running between England and New York, was Paul's next ship. He served on her as second officer for a single voyage, and when both the captain and chief officer died while the ship was in mid-Atlantic, twenty-one-year-old Paul took over the command and safely navigated the *John* into an English port.

Along the waterfront of the British seafaring towns, Captain Paul began to be known as a

careful young skipper who treated his men
fairly, but insisted on harsh discipline, dis-
playing a furious temper when anything went
wrong.

Sailors who had not yet served with him
found such stories hard to believe. Captain
Paul was a little man, not more than five feet
six inches in height. He was slightly built,
brown-haired, and clean-shaven. Some con-
sidered him good-looking, and he encouraged

15

this impression by always dressing extremely smartly when ashore.

Others who studied Paul's face more closely, however, noticed his straight nose and singularly firm chin. There was something about his features—perhaps it was his hard, deep-set eyes—that caused the few friends he had to treat him in a careful and courteous manner. "He'd be a wicked little man to cross," one of them declared. "In a temper, he has the devil in his face."

Paul's conduct at sea soon justified his reputation. While he continued to read Shakespeare and English translations of the ancient Greek classics, he drove his ship in the strictest manner.

At twenty-three years of age, still master of the *John,* he found himself in official trouble for the first time. Mungo Maxwell, the carpenter aboard the vessel, was a troublemaker, and Captain Paul, having no patience for such

men, ordered him to be roped to the mast and given a thorough lashing with the cat-o'-nine-tails.

On arrival in the West Indies, Maxwell complained to the authorities. He then joined another vessel that was sailing for England, and on the voyage home Maxwell caught a fever and died. His family promptly declared that his death was due to the lashing he had received.

When the *John* reached the Scottish port of Kirkcudbright (pronounced Kirkoobry), Paul was arrested and locked up in the local jail. The charge against him was murder.

Within a short time he was released and allowed to make another voyage to the West Indies to obtain written evidence of his innocence. There Paul was able to clear himself completely.

That year of 1770 was a trying one for Paul. Apart from his trouble with the law, the awful climate of the West Indian islands was beginning to affect him. "I have had several severe fevers lately which have reduced me a good deal," he wrote to Mr. Craik in August. "However, I have now completely recovered."

John Paul, Senior, had died in 1767, and in the above letter his son kindly added: "I must beg you to supply my mother should she want anything, as I well know your readiness."

In 1772, when he was only twenty-five years old, Paul obtained the command of a fine, large merchant vessel named the *Betsy*. He drove the ship and her crew hard, spending as little time in port as possible, and looked after the pennies in his careful Scots manner.

Nevertheless, his liking for the sea had diminished. The money he fast was saving was to go toward buying a small plantation in the West Indian island of Tobago. Young Paul very much fancied himself in the role of a fashionable and elegantly dressed young planter.

In 1773, there came into his life a seaman whom afterward he merely referred to as "the ringleader." This loudmouthed bully ruined Paul's career as a British merchant skipper and gave America her famous seaman.

In Tobago trouble arose between Paul and his crew, and it developed into mutiny. When "the ringleader" suddenly charged Captain Paul with a heavy club, Paul thrust at him

with his sword, and the man fell dead on deck.

According to the law, Paul had acted perfectly within his rights, since mutiny was an offense punishable by death. But for some reason that has never been made clear, he decided not to appear in court. Perhaps the dead seaman had many friends in Tobago, and Paul believed they would murder him.

With only $150 in his pockets, Paul hurriedly skipped out of Tobago, made his way to America, and was next heard of in 1774, in the old Quaker city of Philadelphia. "I decided to retire *incognito* to the Continent of America," he wrote to a friend. "And that until the troubles between Britain and the Thirteen Colonies were over, I should remain there."

His friends in America were few, and his brother William recently had died. Paul was hard pressed for money during the next year or two. Vessels sailing along the coast, or from distant seas, came into port at uncertain times and after long and still more uncertain voyages. No shipowner in Philadelphia was able to offer John Paul a job.

Perhaps he was unwilling to produce his seagoing certificates, which were made out in his correct name, for John Paul had changed his name to John Paul Jones. And by that assumed name he was to make his place in the history of America.

In September, distinguished strangers began to appear in Philadelphia. Among them were Christopher Gadsden, of South Carolina; Roger Sherman, of Connecticut; Samuel Adams, of Boston; Henry Lee, of Virginia; and a certain Colonel Washington of Mount Vernon. These men were holding secret meetings in Carpenter's Hall to discuss what was to be done in the event of war.

Although the American colonies were very loyal and very proud to be a part of the British Empire, they were fast losing patience with the meddlesome, second-rate men who governed England at that time. Sheer stupidity and blundering on the part of King George the Third and his political advisers were about to cause the Revolution.

While Jones, in his humble Philadelphia lodging house, continued to mark time, history moved on.

Under a hot June sun in the year 1775, the British Fifty-second Regiment marched shoulder-to-shoulder up the grassy slopes of Bunker Hill. Thirty yards from the summit those splendid troops were shattered by a deadly volley from the twelve hundred muskets of shirtclad farmers, mechanics, and artisans. The American Revolution had begun.

In August, that same year, Joseph Hewes, a congressman from North Carolina, became chairman of the newly formed Marine Committee. His task was to establish an American Navy and to select its officers. Into his office

came a small, hard-eyed, soft-spoken Scotsman who stated that his name was John Paul Jones. He declared that he had had fourteen years' experience on the seas and had sailed as master of several transatlantic vessels. Hewes was impressed by this tough little man who had chosen to fight for America.

Early in December, 1775, John Paul Jones received his commission in the American Navy. At the same time he was appointed first lieutenant aboard a big, lumbering merchant vessel called the *Alfred*. This ship recently had been armed with twenty medium (9-pounder) and ten light (6-pounder) guns.

The *Alfred* was a typical American naval vessel of those days. Until the Revolution began, the colonies had owned not a single warship, and the Marine Committee was therefore forced to hire or buy merchant craft and convert them into vessels of war.

Moreover, there were no trained naval officers or enlisted men. All were civilians whose patriotism had prompted them to join the infant American Navy, and they were totally lacking in experience in naval warfare. The ordinary seamen particularly were disciplined badly.

Away from the wharf beside Walnut Street, Philadelphia, and down the Delaware River went the *Alfred* in January, 1776. Her thirty-dollar-a-month commander was Captain Sal-

tonstall, of Connecticut. Jones, who disliked Saltonstall intensely, was drawing twenty dollars per month, and the 150 seamen aboard the *Alfred* were paid from six to eight dollars a month. The crew's food was, however, much better and more generous than that on British warships. There were ample supplies of beef, pork, potatoes, turnips, peas, butter, cheese, and rice. The butter was a surprising item, since in those days the American colonies produced very little of it.

The *Alfred* put out to sea, accompanied by three smaller vessels, the *Columbus, Cabot,* and *Andrew Doria.* They were in danger at once, for the British Navy was cruising in strong numbers off the American coast.

The Americans dodged the enemy, sailed southward to the British-owned Bahama Islands, and captured, without meeting any resistance, a military fort equipped with large stores of gunpowder, cannon, and iron shot.

They promptly seized these supplies on behalf of the woefully ill-equipped Revolutionary Army.

During the return voyage to the American coast, *Alfred* and her companion ships sighted the British warship *Glasgow,* of twenty guns. What the American vessels lacked in naval experience they made up for in enthusiasm. They piled in from all directions with every muzzle-loaded gun they could bring to bear, banging away at the *Glasgow* in a lusty manner.

The *Alfred* received a heavy battering in return, which disabled her steering. According to Jones:

We received several shot under the water which made the ship very leaky. We had the mainmast shot through and the upper work and rigging very considerably damaged. Yet it is surprising that we only lost

29

the second lieutenant of marines and four men.

Nevertheless, the *Glasgow* was badly out-numbered in terms of men and guns. She took to flight and was unsuccessfully chased by the American ships. Later it was found that she had been so badly damaged that she had to be sent home immediately to England for repairs.

In America there was little rejoicing and a great deal of squabbling over the fight. The general opinion was that the *Glasgow* should have been captured.

Jones himself joined in the argument. In a private letter to Joseph Hewes he accused Captain Saltonstall of being a harsh-spoken bully guilty of "rude, ungentle treatment." For a junior officer to write such a letter was tactless, but Jones still had the alarming habit of saying exactly what he thought. This trait

was to earn him many enemies and few
friends in the American Navy.

In May, 1776, he was placed in command of
a seventy-foot sloop called the *Providence,* a fast,
unstable brute of a ship with a huge fore-and-
aft triangular sail of the same appearance as
that of a modern yacht. When properly han-
dled, she could outrace any square-rigged
vessel. On the other hand, if mishandled she
was quite capable of driving herself directly

into an oncoming wave and drowning the whole crew.

With seventy men and twelve 9-pounder guns Jones streaked out from the Delaware capes in August to do what damage he could to British shipping.

Capturing enemy ships was a profitable occupation for any crew. The system of prize money was originally a British Navy custom, but late in 1776 American naval crews became entitled to a modest share of the money that was received from the sale of a prize vessel.

Within a week Jones had captured the whaling ship *Britannia,* placed officers and men, known as a prize crew, on board, and sent her home to Philadelphia. A few days later he had the misfortune to meet the large British frigate *Solebay,* of twenty-eight guns, which was escorting a convoy of five merchant ships.

The *Solebay* came after *Providence* in a most businesslike manner. One well-aimed broadside from her 9-pounder guns could blow the sloop out of the water.

The New England seamen aboard *Providence* eyed their perky little Scots captain grimly. As far as they were concerned he was a foreigner, and they had not yet learned to trust his judgment.

Jones, with a skill he had learned from handling little sailing boats on the Solway Firth, took the *Providence* tearing across the frigate's bow at a distance of only fifty yards. He then proceeded to outstrip the bigger ship, handling the fast, dangerous *Providence* with miraculous skill.

Captain Symonds of the *Solebay* was so astounded by this maneuver that he forgot to give the order to open fire at the right moment. By the time he recovered, the *Providence* was streaking for the horizon.

Jones wrote:

Our hairbreadth escape and the saucy manner of making it must have annoyed the enemy not a little. He might have fired several broadsides while we were within pistol shot, but he was a bad marksman, and did not hit the *Providence* with one of the many shot which he fired.

Down to the blue sunlit seas off Bermuda raced Jones and his amateur crew. He captured two more valuable prizes, turned north again, dodged another British frigate, and headed for home. On October 8, he sailed into Narragansett Bay with four prizes accompanying him. The three enemy ships he had captured earlier and sent home with prize crews already had arrived safely in American ports.

Although twenty-nine-year-old Captain

1442580

Jones was proving himself a genius at sea, ashore he was proving himself a thorough nuisance to Congress and to the Marine Committee. He continued to write strong and critical letters to everyone he knew. The fact that his views were generally correct did not exactly increase his popularity in official Navy circles.

After his cruise in the *Providence* he wrote:

Our infant Navy is by no means well established, nor under proper regulations. Unless the pay and share of prize money is made equal, if not superior to that of our enemies in these iron times, we cannot hope to repel their force. Can America expect to raise from nothing a navy able to repel the powerful enemy while she pays her own officers and men so poorly?

Jones even stated his strong dislike of the

new naval uniform approved by Congress, which consisted of a blue coat with red lapels, flat gold buttons bearing an embossed anchor, a red waistcoat with gold lace trimming, and blue knee breeches. The hat was in the usual three-cornered style, with a badge affixed on one side.

The uniform was dingy and uninspired, and Jones said so:

> Far better for American officers to be dressed in a uniform much like that of the British Navy. When our ships are sighted by the enemy at close range, a mistake made in judging our nationality may result to our great advantage.

At a meeting with other naval officers, Jones promptly designed another uniform—a dark blue coat with white lapels, a white waistcoat, and white knee breeches and stockings. Since

Congress had not bothered to design any uniform at all for the enlisted men, Jones proceeded to rig them out in a brown jacket and round hat and long pants of the same color.

He even began wearing the smart new naval uniform he had designed. Whenever Captain Jones went ashore, he appeared most neatly dressed. His elegant manners, learned in Scotland and in wealthy West Indian circles, his courteous ways, his soft Scots voice, and his

remarkable knowledge of literature made him a great favorite with hostesses in the polite and cultured society of Boston and Philadelphia. Fashionable and influential ladies declared that Captain Jones was a most modest, accomplished, attractive, and interesting officer. He should, they declared, be given much more say in the running of the American Navy. Jones, of course, fully agreed with their opinion.

What other officers and the members of the Marine Committee thought about such statements is safely left to the imagination. The fact that Captain Jones was as skilled and daring at sea as his admiring civilian friends declared him to be particularly infuriated them. Moreover, he never boasted of his prowess; he was much too clever for that. Shrewdly he believed in the truth of the saying: "Deeds speak louder than words."

Captain Jones went off to sea again at the end of October, 1776. Now he was commanding the big *Alfred,* which Captain Saltonstall had left. With him sailed the little *Providence,* which was now under the command of Captain Hacker.

The two vessels headed for the cold, tempestuous waters off Cape Cod. Among the first prizes they took was the fair-sized *Mellish,* whose holds were filled with warm winter uniforms for the British troops garrisoning chilly Quebec. The ship was hastily sent back under a prize crew, and the uniforms were worn by the American troops that fought under General Washington at the Battle of Trenton.

Jones safely survived a running fight with a big British frigate, the *Milford,* and the *Alfred* was back once more in her home port on December 14.

An amusing insight into the general muddle existing at that time in Congress and in the newly formed Marine Committee is provided by a sentence in Jones's letter that described this voyage: "I paid off the crews of *Alfred* and *Providence* from my own funds and lent the rest of my ready money to Congress."

Captain Jones now made fresh trouble with the Marine Committee. He declared that *Providence* had deserted him at sea and that Captain Hacker should be court-martialed. But since *Providence* had been leaking badly and

41

had lost so many of her crew to man captured British vessels, the committee decided that Captain Hacker's action had been justified. At the same time, Congress informed Jones that it had been decided to relieve him of the command of the *Alfred* and to restore him to the command of the very much smaller *Providence*.

Thereafter, Jones began writing angry letters again. A number of large frigates were being built in American shipyards, and he believed he was entitled to command one of them. He certainly would have made a most capable and daring frigate captain, but Congress did not regard him as an American. The new vessels were to go to native officers such as James Nicholson, of Maryland, John Manley, of Massachusetts, and Dudley Saltonstall, of Connecticut.

Actually Congress treated Captain Jones with reasonable justice. He was the first foreign-born officer to command a vessel of the American Navy. Apparently, however, everyone was growing a little tired of Jones's constant complaints. Nor did his continued success at sea help to increase his popularity with jealous rivals.

In June, 1777, Jones received decisive orders. He was to take charge of a medium-sized warship named the *Ranger,* sail to France on her, and there take command of *L'Indien,* a "fine vessel" twice the size of *Ranger,* which the American commissioners in that country had been ordered to find for him. After trying out the new ship thoroughly, Captain Jones was to sail her home as quickly as possible to America.

Possibly Congress and the Marine Committee were trying to get rid of Jones for a while, having received the following letter from Esek Hopkins, the commander in chief of the American Navy.

I have had from the Officers and people late under Captain Jones's Command a number of Complaints in respect to his Conduct during the Last Cruise. I am well convinced that it will be more difficult to man Vessels under his Command than to do it under any Officer of the Fleet.

The new ship *Ranger,* which had been built at Portsmouth, New Hampshire, beside the Piscataqua River, was square-rigged and three-masted and about 110 feet in length. Her hull was painted black, with a broad yellow stripe running along the sides. She was armed with twenty 9-pounder (3.7 inch) guns, which Jones rightly reduced to eighteen to make the ship more stable.

Not one of the *Ranger's* ten officers, except Captain Parke, of the Marine Corps, had previous naval experience; most of them had been merchant skippers and officers. Among the 140

enlisted sailors were six Irishmen, a French Canadian, two Negroes, and a Scandinavian. They had responded to printed advertisements calling for, in flowery words, "Gentlemen Volunteers who have a Mind to take an agreable (sic) Voyage in this pleasant Season of the Year."

On November 1, 1777, *Ranger* sailed for France. On her way across the Atlantic, Jones sighted and captured a couple of small British

merchantmen. Tearing along through snow, rainstorms, and rough seas, *Ranger* finally reached the French port of Nantes on December 2, accompanied by her two captives. A few days later, in Paris, Jones met the great seventy-year-old Benjamin Franklin, who was the widely known head American commissioner in France.

Dapper Captain Jones liked Paris society. The scented, powdered, and bewigged aristocracy of the royal court of King Louis the Sixteenth approved of his courteous manners and modest habits, and they proceeded to spoil him thoroughly with a constant flood of invitations to dinner, the theater, and formal state receptions.

Who can blame John Paul, the son of a humble Scottish landscape gardener, if all this glittering social success in time went to his head.

During the voyage across the Atlantic, *Ranger* had proved too tender, meaning that she was dangerously unsteady in a rough sea. The *Ranger's* crew, therefore, carried out the tasks of shortening the mainmast, placing thirty tons of ballast in her holds, and procuring a new set of good-quality sails for their vessel while their captain danced and dined in Paris. The harbor now was covered with floating ice, and *Ranger's* deck was deep with snow. The crew began to grumble that this was not "the pleas-

ant Season of the Year" that they had been promised.

The new ship Captain Jones expected was not available, since the American commissioners were short of official funds with which to procure it. Brought up short in his round of enjoyment in Paris by this news, Jones decided to take *Ranger* to sea again and to scour the waters around the British Isles for more enemy merchant ships.

Ranger sailed up the Irish Sea, which divides England from Ireland, on April 18, 1778. There she captured a valuable 250-ton vessel, the *Lord Chatham,* and frightened the life out of the commander of *Hussar,* a British revenue cutter that had to run to save herself. She then spent one night in the English fishing port of Whitehaven.

When Jones announced his intention of burning the town and the small fishing vessels in the harbor, the crew mutinied. Capturing profitable prize ships, in their opinion, was one thing; burning fishermen's boats and houses was another.

Captain Jones, thoroughly accustomed to handling troublesome seamen, merely leveled a pistol at the head of David Cullam, the officer responsible for the mutiny, and threatened to shoot him. The crew quickly went back to work.

The American raiding party landed at dawn on April 23. Some broke into a liquor shop and promptly became drunk on English beer. Meanwhile, Jones and his more daring men ascended the walls of the town's fort, took the sentries prisoner, and proceeded to spike the guns by driving heavy iron wedges into the touchholes. Unfortunately, an Irish sailor from aboard *Ranger* chose this dangerous time to turn traitor. He suddenly began to run through the streets, banging on doors and yelling a warning to the sleeping inhabitants.

As a result, Jones and his party were forced to retreat, and they made their way back to the boats in a cool and deliberate manner. Before they reached *Ranger,* they paused to set fire to a small vessel named the *Thompson.*

About the experience, Jones wrote:

When we had rowed to a considerable distance from the shore, the English began to run in vast numbers to their fort. Their disappointment may be imagined when they found at least thirty heavy cannon rendered useless. Had it been possible to have landed a few hours earlier, my success would have been complete. Not a single ship out of more than 200 could possibly have escaped, and all the world would not have been able to save the town.

What was done, however, is sufficient to show that not all their boasted (British) navy can protect their own shore, and that

the scenes of distress which they have oc-
casioned in America may be soon brought
home to their own door. I was pleased that
in this business we neither killed nor
wounded any person. I brought off three
prisoners as a sample.

Once the men were aboard the *Ranger,* she
scudded across a bright morning sea to the
little rocky headland named St. Mary's Isle.
Since it was within fifteen miles of Mr. Craik's
estate near Arbigland, Jones was familiar with
every foot of the way.

On this peninsula overlooking Solway Firth
stood the fine old brick mansion of the earl of
Selkirk, and Jones intended to kidnap him and
to hold him for ransom. He believed that the
British government would do almost anything
to restore the earl to freedom.

The idea was not very bright. Selkirk was a
pleasant gentleman, who grew roses, told his

children delightful fairy tales, and was not at all important to the British government or anyone else. Indeed, King George the Third barely knew he existed.

After covering the twenty miles to St. Mary's Isle, Jones went ashore in a boat, accompanied by two officers and a dozen well-armed sailors. About half-past ten, they managed to reach the house without being detected.

Unfortunately, the earl was away from home, but his wife and children were still at the breakfast table. The countess suddenly noticed the "horrid-looking wretches" in her garden and believed they were pirates. With aristocratic good manners she welcomed them into her house. The two officers informed her that they were from the American ship *Ranger* and that they had been ordered to carry away the household silver. Neither of them appeared either proud or happy, according to the countess, to carry out this order. Both of them, she

declared, behaved in a civil and courteous manner.

The raiding party retreated to the shore, carrying the earl's household plate in a couple of sacks. Included with the silver trays and forks and spoons was the breakfast teapot, with the warm tea leaves still in it.

While *Ranger* sailed away, the countess wrote to Mr. Craik, informing him that the man who had raided her home was John Paul, "born in your grounds and a gardener's son of yours. We were perfectly unacquainted with him till his landing at my house."

On her homeward voyage to France, *Ranger* was sighted by the British naval ship *Drake,* which was a little smaller and more lightly gunned than the American vessel. They clashed off the coast of northeast Ireland, with hundreds of delighted Irishmen lining the shores to watch the fight.

After a "warm, close, and obstinate fight" lasting two hours, Captain Burden and the chief officer of *Drake* were killed, whereupon the crew surrendered. Jones placed a prize crew aboard the captured ship. Both vessels returned to France via the west coast of Ireland and reached port safely on May 8.

While Jones sat in his cabin writing a polite and overlong letter of apology to Lady Selkirk for the removal of her silverware, the British naval authorities and government were almost

CRUISE OF THE *RANGER* 1778

dancing with fury. For seven hundred years no enemy had dared to set foot on British soil. An American rebel now had done so. Moreover, he had captured a British naval vessel within British territorial waters.

The *London Morning Chronicle* sportingly declared:

> The *Drake* was a smaller ship, but in engagements with the French and Spaniards, such a difference would have been unimportant. But the case is different when we engage with our own countrymen; men who have the same spirit and bravery as ourselves.

The ordinary British people, who have always greatly admired anyone who administers a good kick to authority and tradition, grinned as they spoke of Captain Jones. They decided rightly that his daring adventure might do a great deal to wake up the British government and the British admiralty. In any case, many of them thought that King George the Third never should have gone to war with the American colonies. They also hoped that poor Lady Selkirk got back her teapot and the rest of the loot. She did; Captain Jones returned every piece of it after the war.

Back in France, Jones proceeded to squabble with the authorities over the sale of *Drake*, the division of prize money, and the lack of a new and bigger warship for himself. He also squabbled with his crew, kicking one midshipman down the poop ladder and placing another in irons for breaking a thermometer in his cabin.

For the rest of 1778, and well into 1779, Jones was left in France. Congress made a most serious mistake in not using his capable services, for the American Navy was passing through a disastrous period. Their frigate *Ran-*

dolph was blown up and sunk by the British Navy, and frigate *Virginia* was wrecked when it went ashore on the American coast. *Hancock* and *Delaware,* two more frigates, were captured by the British. A number of other ill-spared vessels also met with similar kinds of misfortune.

In August, 1779, Jones received command of the three-masted, square-rigged *Bon Homme Richard,* a ship much more in keep-

ing with his high esteem of his own qualities. She was a large but ancient French merchant ship that had formerly been in the East Indian trade. King Louis the Sixteenth of France had placed this nine-hundred-ton vessel at Captain Jones's disposal.

One way or another, Jones managed to arm the *Bon Homme Richard* with a total of forty guns. There were six 9-pounders (3.7 inches), twenty-eight 12-pounders (4.5 inches), and six long and heavy 18-pounders (5.3 inches), which were normally deadly weapons that could destroy a ship. Those that Captain Jones obtained, however, were old and of uncertain quality.

Another important step he took was to make sure he engaged a good crew. The *Ranger*, with her grumbling and mutinous crowd of "spoilt boys," had all sailed home to America under a Lieutenant Simpson. The new crew of the *Bon Homme Richard* numbered 374 all told, and they were disciplined veterans of different nationalities. Most of the 17 officers were American, but out of 43 petty officers 27 of them were British deserters. Of the 144 seamen, 46 were American, 54 British (also deserters), and the rest Portuguese, Scandinavians, and Scots. In addition, there were 170 French Marines, some of whom at least were armed with the latest rifled muskets instead of the more usual inaccurate smoothbore weapons.

When the *Bon Homme Richard* left France on August 14, 1779, four other war vessels accompanied her. They were the new American-built frigate *Alliance,* which had been attached for duty with the French Navy, the frigate *La Pallas,* of French nationality, *La Vengeance,* a smaller and lighter corvette, and a speedy little dispatch boat that had been named *Le Cerf.*

Alliance was under the command of a certain French captain named Pierre Landais. Although an experienced seaman, he was undoubtedly mad, and Congress had made the mistake of granting Landais a commission in the American Navy. The other vessels were commanded by extremely competent French officers.

Jones's squadron sailed up the west coast of Ireland, capturing prizes as they went. *Le Cerf* went astray in a storm and finally made her way back to France alone. Around the cold and bleak shores of the Orkney Islands to the north of Scotland went the *Bon Homme Richard* and her three companion vessels. Several more enemy ships fell into the hands of the squadron and were sent back promptly to French ports.

Captain Landais then began to become unhinged. He talked to himself, flew into violent rages, and was suspicious of his own crew, of Jones, and of everyone else.

After failing, through bad weather, to raid and hold for ransom the Scottish town of Leith on the east coast, Jones continued his southerly course between England and the Continent. Off the grassy gray cliffs of England's Flamborough Head on September 23, 1779, the *Bon Homme Richard* sighted a convoy of forty-one British ships approaching. Escorting this fleet of merchant ships were the enemy frigate *Serapis*, which carried forty-four guns, and the smaller *Countess of Scarborough*, which carried twenty guns.

Captain Richard Pearson of the *Serapis* was proud of his ship. She was a new, fast vessel, carrying a main battery of twenty 18-pounder guns, apart from numerous 9- and 6-pounders. On sighting Captain Jones's squadron, Pearson ordered the merchant ships under his command to make for safety under the guns of a coastal fort. Accompanied by the *Countess* he then steered straight for the *Bon Homme Richard*.

67

The sea was almost a flat calm, and there was practically no breeze.

At six o'clock on that sunny evening the first shots were exchanged. Two of Jones's old 18-pounder guns burst almost at once, killing members of the crew and putting the other four 18-pounders out of action. Similar heavy weapons aboard the *Serapis* soon began to smash into the *Bon Homme Richard* in deadly salvos.

Jones realized that he must run close alongside the *Serapis* and try to board her. If he remained at a distance, the British vessel would tear his ship to bits with her fast and accurate shooting.

He actually brought *Bon Homme Richard* against the hull of the *Serapis,* so that the two ships were parallel, but facing in opposite directions. Pearson realized that he was now at a disadvantage. Only by keeping at a distance from the *Bon Homme Richard* could he be sure of destroying her with his long-range guns. He therefore gave the order to anchor *Serapis,* hoping that, in the very light breeze, the *Bon Homme Richard* would begin to drift away from his ship.

By this time, however, the rigging of the two ships had become interlocked, and Jones ordered both vessels to be lashed together with strong cables. In a kind of deadly dance the two ships continued to swing round and round, side by side, while their guns fired into each other's hull at absolutely point-blank range. In the wild fury of battle, Captain Jones himself helped to serve one of the ship's 9-pounder guns.

Meanwhile, the French ship *La Pallas* had sturdily engaged the *Countess of Scarborough.* The little *La Vengeance* scuttled around on the outskirts of the fight like a timid old lady. Captain Landais of *Alliance* apparently then went completely mad. He sailed within fifty yards of the

Bon Homme Richard, his own companion vessel, and gave the order for a broadside to be fired into her. He repeated this murderous trick twice more, making three broadsides altogether.

This action "killed a number of men," stated American officers of Jones's ship at the court-martial, which was held at a later date. "It dismounted sundry guns, put out the side lights, and silenced all the 12-pounders."

Both the *Serapis* and the *Bon Homme Richard* were now battered, wreathed in smoke, and on fire in different places. Dead and wounded men covered their decks. It was at this stage that brave Captain Pearson hailed Jones with the goading question: "Has your ship surrendered?"

The equally brave Jones, grimy with smoke, dazed by the roar of the guns, and scorched by the repeated discharges of his own 9-pounder, shouted back over the din of battle his famous,

immortal reply: "I have not yet begun to fight."

The time was then about 8 p.m., and the furious, deadly battle continued for another two hours, the huge rolling clouds of smoke completely blotting out the light of the full moon. During that time, a dazed petty officer aboard *Bon Homme Richard* began yelling to *Serapis* that his vessel desired to surrender. Jones immediately pulled a pistol from his belt and hurled it at the man, knocking him down. But Captain Pearson had heard the man's cries.

"Sir, do you ask for quarter?" he shouted to him.

"No, sir," replied Jones. "I haven't yet thought of it, but I'm determined to make *you* surrender."

At 10:30 p.m. the mainmast of the *Serapis* fell with a thunderous crash. Soon afterward Captain Pearson surrendered. The appalling sea battle lasted almost four hours before the end came.

Bon Homme Richard had been shot to pieces and was in danger of sinking. Jones and his crew were later forced to transfer to the captured *Serapis*. A number of his men were also detailed to go aboard the *Countess of Scarborough,* which *La Pallas* had pounded into surrender. The entire squadron, including the two captured vessels, slowly made their way to the

74

coast of Holland. Behind them, the gallant old *Bon Homme Richard* finally went down.

During this battle, 150 of Jones's men had been killed and wounded. *Serapis* lost almost the same number.

While France was applauding Jones as a great naval fighter, British Navy vessels were furiously searching the seas for him. But the ordinary British people composed fresh ballads in his honor and promptly made him a popular hero, much to the great anger of King George and his worthless crowd of statesmen. At this time, England was in a state of uproar, and her leaders were calling on their lazy and incompetent government to resign.

Landais went back to America to face a court-martial, which passed the sentence: "The said Peter Landais to be broke and rendered incapable of serving in the American Navy for the future."

In late December, Jones and his ships escaped back to France, and he remained there until the autumn of 1780. Congress had not paid his salary since he had arrived in that country almost three years earlier. Furthermore, endless arguments with the French authorities held up much of the prize money to which he and his men were entitled. He managed to collect only a portion of the cash before he was ordered to take command of the smaller ex-British naval vessel *Ariel*. This ship

CRUISE OF THE *BON HOMME RICHARD* 1779

SHETLAND ISLES

September 1

ORKNEY ISLES

August 28

SCOTLAND

September 15

NORTH SEA

Solway Firth

IRELAND

IRISH SEA

Battle with *Serapis*
September 23, 1779
Flamborough Head

October 3

TEXEL

WALES

ENGLAND

December 1779

August 23

ENGLISH CHANNEL

August 16

FRANCE

carried a heavy cargo of supplies urgently needed by Washington's army.

Jones sailed from France in October, 1780. On his way across the Atlantic he fought an indecisive battle with the British ship *Triumph,* which finally took to her heels. On February 18, 1781, he arrived at Philadelphia after an absence of more than three years. He had fought his last battle under the American flag.

By this time, most of the American Navy vessels had been captured or destroyed. Others had been trapped in bays and harbors by British warships. With the end of the war in sight, Jones began planning to settle down, and he made several efforts to obtain small country estates. For one reason or another, however, the deals came to nothing. Probably he was not too keen on remaining in America, having grown to love the gay, colorful life of Paris and the cultured ways of the French people.

American independence was acknowledged in Britain in November, 1781, and formal peace was declared in September, 1783. In November, 1783, Congress authorized Captain Jones to proceed to France and negotiate with the French government for the handing over to American seamen of the large sums of prize money still outstanding after the conclusion of the war.

For three years Jones remained in Paris, where he was still regarded as a popular hero. His gay social life helped to compensate for all the trouble and delays he experienced in trying to secure prize money that was owed him from the niggly and somewhat dishonest French authorities.

In the summer of 1787, he returned to America, bringing with him the money he had managed to obtain. But by this time forty-year-old Jones seemed to have lost much of his affection for this country. He made no further

efforts to buy land or to settle in any kind of business. The glittering life of Paris called to him once again from across the wide Atlantic Ocean.

Uninterested in politics, Jones did not guess that France was on the verge of a great revolution that would sweep away the aristocratic society he had enjoyed so much in past years. Before the end of 1787, he had left America for the last time.

Back in France, Jones wrote with obvious satisfaction:

I was received by the King and his ministers as a general officer and a special minister from Congress. I went to Court much oftener than our (American) minister.

Jones had thrown away the good acres of American soil he might easily have obtained in exchange for the glittering but worthless existence of the French court, which, in any case, was soon to perish. He had made the greatest mistake of his life.

In the year 1789, when Washington was elected first president of the United States, the French Revolution began. Almost overnight, Paris became a city of anarchy and terror. But by that time, Captain Jones had become Kontradmiral Pavel Ivanovitch, or rear admiral, in the Russian Imperial Navy.

Sixty-year-old Catherine the Second, Empress of Russia, was a shocking old woman in many ways, but she was a capable ruler. She had succeeded to the throne by the simple process of arranging to have her former husband, the Emperor Peter the Third, quietly murdered. Later she had begun enlarging Russia's southern border by attempting to make the Black Sea a "Russian lake" and the Turkish city of Constantinople (modern Istanbul) a Russian frontier city. Naturally the Turks objected.

The Russian Black Sea Fleet was a strange collection of queer little ships that mounted all kinds of guns and were officered by adventurers of many different nations. Catherine believed that a capable and senior naval officer was required to hammer this collection of ships into a worthwhile fighting unit. The Turkish ships were no better than the Russian ones, but their crews displayed a more fiery fighting spirit and better seamanship than the Cossacks, slaves, river boatmen, and incompetent princes of Catherine's own fleet. Who could improve her navy quicker and better than the world famous American officer Captain John Paul Jones?

On a salary of $145 per month, Jones took over his naval duties in the Black Sea, where he arrived in May, 1788. He soon saw for himself that the Russian fleet was exactly as a

French officer had described it: "A motley collection of detestable boats of all sizes and shapes, armed by men who were neither sailors, soldiers, nor officers, but Russians and no cowards."

The fleet was under the supreme command of a Dutch-German named Prince Nassau-Siegen. A handsome fellow, with a tremendous opinion of himself, he was, however, utterly incompetent and therefore jealous of Jones. All-powerful and brutal Prince Potemkin, commander in chief of the Russian armed forces, cared little or nothing for Jones either. A Greek named Alexiano, one of the top naval commanders, was also extremely jealous. Admiral Voinovitch shared Alexiano's views and almost totally ignored Jones. The feelings of all these foreign officers became even more bitter as in crazy, skirmishing fights against the more numerous Turkish fleet Jones proved that he was undoubtedly the most competent naval officer of all those in the Empress Catherine's service.

One night he set out in a small rowboat with a sturdy Russian seaman named Ivak at the oars. He spent several hours being rowed in and out among the unsuspecting anchored Turkish vessels in order to obtain an idea of their strength. Across the stern of one powerful enemy gunboat he wrote in chalk: "This ship to be burned. Paul Jones." And burned the vessel was in the sea battle that took place the following morning.

Years later, Ivak showed a British officer a handsome dagger that had been inscribed with the words: "From Pavel Jones to his friend Cossack Ivak."

Ivak told his visitor, "Never in my life have I seen such a man as he was. When he liked, he could be honey. But when angry, he could be like a stone." In fact, all the Russian officers who served with Jones admired his skill

THIS SHIP
TO BE BURNED Paul Jones

and daring, and many of them wrote and spoke openly in his favor.

In October of 1788, he was relieved of his command, and he went to the Russian capital city of St. Petersburg (now called Leningrad) to await further orders from the Empress. There his good name was smeared by his jealous rivals and his reputation with the Empress ruined. At the end of 1789, Jones was in Amsterdam, Holland, and in the following year he returned to Paris. By that time he was becoming very short of funds.

Thomas Carlyle, a famous British author, wrote about him:

Poor Jones. In faded naval uniform, he lingers visible here; like a wine-skin from which the wine is drawn. Like the ghost of himself! Poor Paul! Hunger and dispiritment track thy sinking footsteps; once or at most twice, in the Revolutionary tumult

the figure of thee emerges; mute, ghost-like.

It is sad to relate that during these last two years of his life, the great Captain Jones became a bore to his few remaining friends and perhaps slightly affected in the head. He wrote long and windy letters to his acquaintances. He still haunted the vast, but now deserted, drawing rooms of the aristocracy, the theaters, and the homes he had known in the vanished days of royalty, but he lived in cheap lodgings, which he barely managed to pay for with his remaining money.

Snobbish Gouverneur Morris, American minister to France, coldly noted in his diary on November 14, 1790: "Paul Jones calls on me. He has nothing to say, but is so kind as to bestow on me all the Hours which hang heavy on his Hands."

In June, 1792, Congress belatedly remembered her great sailor of the Revolution, and Captain John Paul Jones was appointed a special American representative to the Sultan's Court at Algiers. Although the salary was not outstanding, the appointment meant that Jones would once again hold a dignified and respected position. But the letter with this news did not reach Paris until the middle of August. And on July 18, 1792, a month before the letter arrived, forty-five-year-old Captain Jones died of bronchial pneumonia in his lonely lodgings.

The revolutionary government that now ruled France made sure that he was given a ceremonious funeral. Frenchmen, whatever their politics, had not forgotten his brilliant naval record. A squad of smartly uniformed soldiers marched at the head of the procession. They were followed by carriages containing prominent French politicians and a few of the Captain's faithful friends—old seamen, soldiers, and those citizens of Paris who had known Captain John Paul Jones in his great days.

Gouverneur Morris could not be bothered to attend; he had to prepare for a dinner party he was giving that evening. In any case, he seldom had any time for men who had become failures.

The coffin was laid to rest on July 20 in a Protestant cemetery outside the walls of Paris. There it remained, forgotten and overlooked, for 113 years, until General Horace Porter,

American ambassador to France, spent a great deal of time and money searching for the grave. In July, 1905, USS *Brooklyn* conveyed the coffin across the Atlantic Ocean. With the greatest of naval ceremonies, including the firing of salutes by the guns of splendid American warships, Captain John Paul Jones returned to his adopted country.

His coffin finally was laid to rest in the crypt of the chapel of the United States Naval Academy at Annapolis. No more suitable spot could have been chosen, for during his lifetime Captain Jones repeatedly had urged the building of this naval academy.

Nor had Britain forgotten Captain John Paul Jones, whose daring raids on her coast and gallant battle against His Majesty's Ship *Serapis* had set the entire country in an uproar. A later generation of British historians had come to regard him as a great and daring naval captain. The old ballads of his wonderful ad-

ventures were still remembered in out-of-the-way parts of England.

In the year 1940, when a weak and battered Britain defiantly faced a hostile Germany across the twenty-mile strip of the English Channel, the First Lord of the Admiralty declared in a broadcast to America: "In the words of your own great seaman, Captain Paul Jones, Britain has not yet begun to fight."

Bibliography

Cooper, James Fenimore, *History of the Navy of the United States of America.* Paris: Baudry's European Library, 1839.

De Koven, Anna F., *The Life and Letters of John Paul Jones.* New York: Charles Scribner's Sons, 1913.

Lodge, Henry C., *The Story of the Revolution.* New York: Charles Scribner's Sons, 1898.

Lorenz, Lincoln, *John Paul Jones: Fighter for Freedom and Glory.* Annapolis, Maryland: United States Naval Institute, 1943.

Morison, Samuel Eliot, *John Paul Jones: A Sailor's Biography.* Boston: Little, Brown and Company, 1959.

Ronald Syme spent his boyhood in New Zealand. At sixteen he left school and went to sea in a Pacific cargo steamer. At eighteen, he began writing short stories, and in 1934 he left the sea to become a professional writer. During World War II Mr. Syme served in the British Merchant Service as a gunner until he was transferred to the British Army Intelligence Corps.

Today Mr. Syme is a well-known author in both England and the United States. He lives in Rarotonga in the Cook Islands of the South Pacific, and he is married to the niece of the paramount chieftain there. His home is a white-walled stone house standing within two hundred yards of a beautiful lagoon and surrounded by palm trees. He uses one large room of this house exclusively as his office. The shelves are lined with books, and Mr. Syme can check almost any historical fact he needs for his writing in his library. He enjoys, as he says, "most of the comforts of civilization without the corresponding disadvantages."